Bradwell

BOOK

Wit & H

# THE BRITS DOWN SOUTH

### CAULDON GREY
POKES FUN AT HIS FRIENDS DOWN SOUTH

BRADWELL
**BOOKS**

Published by Bradwell Books
9 Orgreave Close Sheffield S13 9NP
Email: books@bradwellbooks.co.uk
Compiled by Cauldon Grey

British Library Cataloguing in Publication Data: a catalogue record for
this book is available from the British Library.
1st Edition
ISBN: 9781910551295


Design & Typeset by: Jenks Design
Illustrations: ©Tim O'Brien 2016
Back cover cartoon. © Chris Horlock 2016
Print: Hobbs the Printers, Totton Hants

*"The North and South have a love/hate relationship; Southerners love themselves and Northerners hate them for it."* **Anon**

**A cockney went** to the doctor's.
"I think I'm a kleptomaniac, doc," he says, "Can you help me?"

"Take these pills," says the GP, "and if they don't work in two weeks, get me a flat screen telly."

**A Millwall fan** appeared in court one day charged with disorderly conduct and assault. The arresting officer stated that the accused had thrown something into the river.

"What exactly did the accused throw?" the judge asked.
"Stones, sir," replied the police officer.

"Well, that's hardly an offence is it?" said the judge irritably.
"It was in this case, sir," said the officer, "Stones was the referee."

**At a local** derby between Arsenal and Spurs, a spectator suddenly found himself in the thick of dozens of flying bottles.

"There's nothing to worry about, mate," said the elderly chap standing next to him.

"It's like the bombs during the war. You won't get hit unless the bottle's got your name on it."

"That's just what I'm worried about," said the fan, "my name's John Smith."

**A man and** his wife were sitting in their living room in south London and he said to her, "Just so you know, love, I never want to live in a vegetative state, dependent on some machine and fluids from a bottle. If that ever happens, just pull the plug."

His wife got up, unplugged the TV and threw out all of his lager.

**A Yorkshireman walks** into a bank in Knightsbridge and says to the female cashier, "I want to open a current account now!" The lady replied, "I beg your pardon, sir, what did you say?" "Listen cloth-ears," snapped the man aggressively, "I said I want to open a current account right now!"

"Sir, I'm sorry," said the flustered cashier, "but we do not tolerate rudeness to staff in this bank." The assistant left the window, went over to the bank manager and complained to him about her customer. They both returned and the manager spoke sternly to the aggressive customer, "What seems to be the problem here?"

"There's no problem," replied the Yorkshire man, "I just won 50 million in the lottery and I want to open a current account in this bank right now!" "I see, sir," the manager said, "and this silly woman is giving you a hard time, is she?"

**A professor at** the London School of Economics met his new class on the first day of term. He stood before them and gave a nice introduction about himself. He finished his monologue, looked around the room and asked his students, "If any of you think you are stupid, stand up."

He looked around and saw that none of his students had stood up. He proceeded to ask the same question again, "If anyone thinks they are stupid, please stand up."

The professor looked around and to his surprise one student, a tall lad from Bolton, was standing up at the back of the class.

"Do you think you are stupid?" the professor asked.
"No," the lad replied, "I just didn't want you to feel alone."

**In a remote** convent on the Dorset coast, the 98-year-old Mother Superior lay dying. The nuns gathered around her bed, trying to make her last days comfortable. They gave her some fresh warm milk to drink from their own dairy cow. She turned her face away, refusing to drink it.

One of the nuns took the glass back to the kitchen and she remembered that the previous Christmas a grateful visitor had given the convent a bottle of single-malt whisky. She opened it and poured a generous amount into the warm milk. Back at Mother Superior's bed, she held the glass to her lips. The old nun drank a little, then a little more and before they knew it she had drunk the whole glass down to the last drop.

"Mother," the nuns asked earnestly, "please give us some wisdom before you die."

The Mother Superior raised herself up in bed and, with a pious look on her face, said, "Don't sell that cow!"

**Little Brad in** Whitehaven phones his uncle in Somerset and says, "Thanks for the harmonica you gave me for my birthday. It's the best present I ever got."

"That's great," said his uncle. "So you know how to play it well then?"

"Oh, I don't play it," little Brad replied. "My mum gives me a fiver a week not to play it during the day, and my dad gives me a fiver a week not to play it at night!"

**A young banker** in London decided to get his first tailor-made suit from Saville Row. As he tried it on, he reached down to put his hands in the pockets but to his surprise found none.

He mentioned this to the tailor, a Geordie, who asked him, "You're a banker, right?"

The young man answered, "Yes, I am."

"Well, whoever heard of a banker putting his hand in his pocket?"

**A cockney moves** to Scunthorpe and applies for a job as a handyman.

At the interview, his future boss asks, "Can you do electrics, lad?" "Oh no, mate," says the cockney.

"But you can do carpentry?" says the governor.

"No, mate, no carpentry," says the cockney.

"Well, how about plumbing then?" the guv asks, getting a bit tetchy.

"Oh, no, mate," says the cockney, "I don't know nuffink about plumbing." "You're not very handy then, are you?" says the boss.

"Yes, of course I am, mate," says the cockney, "I live round the corner."

**Cockney:** "I'm thinking and I have a question for you – why have women never been to the moon?"

**His mate:** "I don't rightly know. Why have women never been to the moon?"

**Cockney:** "Because it never needed cleaning."

**A glamorous woman** from Bath was out shopping in the Salford Shopping Centre when she was accosted by a dirty, shabby-looking homeless woman who asked her for a couple of pounds for food.

The woman took out her purse, extracted ten pounds and asked, "If I give you this money, will you buy some wine with it instead of food?"

"No, I had to stop drinking years ago," the homeless woman replied somewhat surprised.

"Will you use it to go clothes shopping instead of buying food?" the woman asked. "No, I don't waste time shopping," the homeless woman said. "I need to spend all my time trying to stay alive."

"Will you spend it at a beauty salon then instead of buying food?" the woman asked.

"Are you NUTS?!" exclaimed the homeless woman. "I haven't had my hair done in twenty years!" "Well," said the woman, "I'm not going to give you the money. Instead, I'm going to take you out for dinner with my hubby and myself tonight."

The homeless woman was astounded. "Won't your husband be furious with you for doing that?" she asked, "I know I'm dirty, and I probably smell pretty disgusting."

"That's okay," replied the woman from Bath, "It's important for him to see what a woman looks like after she has given up shopping, hair appointments and wine."

**A titled gentleman** from the South once bought a big estate in Lancashire. He summoned the cook.

"I am planning a great entertainment to welcome my friends," he announced, "and I want none of your disgusting local offal on the menu: no black pudding, no tripe, no pigs' trotters nor oxtail."

The cook nodded wondering what his fancy guests could eat.
"You will serve oysters, caviar, duck livers and frogs' legs."
"Yes, milord," said the cook, "And will the gentlefolk be requiring basins or buckets after?"

**A man from** London was visiting his friend in York. They were having tea when the Londoner coughed violently, and his false teeth shot across the room and smashed against the wall.

"Oh, dear," he said, "Whatever shall I do? I can't afford a new set."

"Don't worry, lad," said his friend. "I'll get a pair from me sister for you." bThe next day the Yorkshireman came back with the teeth, which fitted perfectly.

"This is wonderful," said the Londoner. "Your sister must be a very good dentist."

"Oh, she's not a dentist," replied his friend, "she's an undertaker. Waste not want not."

**A young man,** obviously from the upper class, was standing just outside the door of London's Dorchester Hotels, idly puffing at a cigarette, when he was approached by a man in a cloth cap who was down from Consett to work on a building site. The northerner said to the young man, "I bet your father's stinking rich."

"Extremely rich," said the upper-class fellow arrogantly.

"And I suppose all your life, you've never wanted for owt, had everything you want like," said the Consett man.

"Just about," said the upper class man smugly.

"And you've never done a single day's work in your life."

"I'm afraid that's so."

The northerner thought it over and said, "Well, you haven't missed a thing."

**A Londoner and** his 'bird' Sharon are walking down Oxford Street one night. She sees a necklace in a window of a jewellers and says, "Oh, Darren, I'd love that!" so Darren throws a brick through the window and gives her the necklace.

A bit further down, she sees a handbag in a clothes shop window and says, "Oh, Darren, I'd REALLY love that!" so Darren throws a brick through the window of the shop and hands her the handbag.

Further along she stops outside a shoe shop and says, "Ooh, Darren I'd REALLY REALLY love those!" and Darren says, "What's the matter with you Sharon, do you think I'm made of bricks?"

**Q:** How do southerners get jobs?

**A:** They ask daddy.

**Q:** What do you call a car crash in Knightsbridge?

**A:** A crèche.

**Q:** What's the first question at a cockney quiz night?

**A:** 'What you lookin' at?'

**A Yorkshireman pulled** up outside a hotel in the West End of London in a cab.

"That'll be £5.00, guv," said the taxi-driver.

"'Appen I've only got 4 quid, lad," said the Yorkshireman, "Can tha back up a bit?"

**Q:** What's the difference between a City of London investment banker and a pigeon?

**A:** The pigeon is still capable of leaving a deposit on a new Maserati.

**A party of** southerners are climbing in the Lake District. After several hours they became hopelessly lost. One of them studied the map for some time, turning it this way and that, up and down, identifying distant landmarks, consulting his compass, noting the direction of the sun. Finally he said, "OK, you see that big mountain over there? Scafell Pike?"

"Yes," answered the others eagerly.

"Well, according to the map, we're standing on top of it."

**When Albert** from the Grimethorpe Colliery band came back from his first trip to London, everyone in Barnsley was keen to find out how he had got on. "Did tha like it, lad?" asked his mates in the brass band. "Oh, it wasn't bad," said Albert.

"As good as that, was it?" said his friends.

"Well, there was just the one thing wrong. The other guests in hotel just would not go to bed." Albert shook his head, bemused. "They were in the corridor outside me room shouting and banging on t' door until three o'clock in t' morning every night."

"So what did tha do, Albert?" asked the villagers.

"Well," he replied, "I just kept on playing me tuba."

**Charlton were playing** Derby County when Charlton centre-forward took a knock to the head and was laid out on the pitch. His manager came running over just as the player regained consciousness.

"He doesn't know his own name," said the medic, "He's got no idea who he is."

"That's okay," said the manager, "Tell him he's Pele and send him back on."

**Andy from Enfield** was working as a security guard at a big factory on the outskirts of Manchester. He was on duty one day when he spotted a worker walking out of the factory gates pushing a wheelbarrow with a suspicious-looking package in it. The guard stopped the bloke, opened the package up and found it contained nothing but some sawdust and floor-sweepings.

The next day the guard stopped the same worker who was again pushing a wheelbarrow containing a suspicious-looking package. Once again it contained nothing but some sawdust and floor-sweepings.

The same thing happened for several days on the trot. Andy was getting really frustrated – that crafty northerner was up to something, he thought. Finally Andy stopped the worker and said, "OK, I give up. I know you are up to something, but I can't tell what."

The worker smirked and said nothing.

"Please, I promise not to turn you in, but put me out of my misery – tell me what you are stealing."

"Alright, mate," laughed the crafty Mancunian, "I'm stealing wheelbarrows."

**At a school** in South Kensington, the teacher announces a new classroom initiative.

"Good morning, children, each Thursday we're going to have a general knowledge quiz. The pupil who gets the answer right can have Friday and Monday off and not come back to school until Tuesday."

Wee Jackie, who has just moved to London from the Scottish Borders, thinks, "Aye, man. Ah'm pure dead brilliant at ma general knowledge stuff an' that. This is gonnae be a doddle; it's a lang weekend fur me."

The teacher says, "Right, class, who can tell me who said, 'Don't ask what your country can do for you, but what you can do for your country?'"

Wee Jackie shoots up his hand, waving furiously in the air. Teacher looks round and picks Jeremy at the front. "Yes, Jeremy?"

Jeremy says in his very posh English accent, "Yes, miss, the answer is J F Kennedy in his inauguration speech in 1960."
"Very good, Jeremy," says the teacher, "You may stay off on Friday and Monday and we will see you back in class on Tuesday."

The next Thursday comes around, and Wee Jackie is even more determined.

The teacher asks, "Who said. 'We will fight them on the beaches, we will fight them in the air, we will fight them at sea. But we will never surrender?'"

Wee Jackie's hand shoots up, arm stiff as a board, shouting, "I know. I know, Me Miss, me Miss!"

Teacher looks round and picks Timothy, sitting at the front, "Yes, Timothy?"

Timothy says in a very, very posh English accent, "The answer is Winston Churchill, Miss, in his 1941 Battle of Britain speech." "Very good, Timothy," says the teacher, "you may stay off on Friday and Monday and come back to class on Tuesday."

The following Thursday comes around and Wee Jackie is hyper. He's been studying encyclopedias all week and he's ready for anything that comes.

The teacher asks, "Who said 'One small step for man, one giant leap for mankind'?"

Wee Jackie's arm shoots straight in the air; he's standing on his seat, jumping up and down screaming, "Miss, me miss, meeeeee!"

The teacher looks round the class and picks Rupert, sitting at the front. "Yes Rupert?"

Rupert replies in a frightfully, frightfully, ever so plumy English accent, "Yes, Miss, that was Neil Armstrong. 1969, the first moon landing."

"Very good, Rupert," says the teacher. "You may stay off on Friday and Monday and come back into class on Tuesday."
Wee Jackie loses the plot altogether, tips his desk over and throws his little chair at the wall. He starts screaming, "Fur God's sake, where did all these stuck up English so-and-sos come from?"

The teacher looks round the class, "Who said that?"

Wee Jackie grabs his blazer and his satchel and heads for the door, "Sir William Wallace, Battle of Falkirk, July 1298, See yous on Tuesday!!"

**In a large** stately home in Lancashire, an extremely wealthy man is on his death bed and he calls for his longest serving servants, one from Clithero the other Lytham St. Ann's and his chauffeur from Uxbridge.

"Chef," he says, "You have been with me for many years and made me some of the nicest meals I've ever had. To you, I shall leave Toff Hall. It has 75 rooms and a large garden. I hope you enjoy it as much as I enjoyed your food."

"Thank you, sir," says Chef and he leaves the room. The wealthy man turns to his butler. "Jeeves, you have always been here attending to my every whim at all hours of the day and night for all these years. To you, I shall leave Posh Hall. It has 100 rooms, tennis courts, a large garden and a helipad. I hope it serves you as well as you have served me."

"Thank you, sir," says Jeeves and he leaves the room.

The wealthy man turns to James, his chauffeur, with a grim expression.

"And finally you, James. You, sir, are a disgrace. You were never there when I needed you and when you were the car was dirty with empty beer bottles and old cigarette ends all over the interior. I even found some black lace panties on the back seat once. To you, I shall leave damn all.

" James nods. "So how many rooms does that one have?" he asks.

**A Yorkshireman and** his date walk into a very posh furrier in London's Bond Street. "Show the lady your finest mink!" orders the Yorkshireman.

So the rather snotty shop assistant goes in the back and comes out with an absolutely gorgeous full-length mink coat. As the lady tries it on, the salesman sidles up to the Yorkshireman and discreetly whispers, "Ah, sir, that particular fur goes for £65,000." "No problem, lad," says the Yorkshireman, "I'll write you a cheque."

"Very good, sir," says the smarmy shop assistant, thinking of his commission. "Today is Saturday so you may come by on Monday to pick it up after the bank has cleared the cheque." So the Yorkshireman and his very happy date leave the furriers arm-in-arm.

On Monday, the Yorkshireman returns. The sales assistant is outraged.

"How dare you show your face in here!" he splutters, "There wasn't a single penny in your bank account! Your cheque bounced. You've got a damn cheek!"

"Aye, lad," grinned the Yorkshireman, "but I just had to come by to thank you for the best weekend of my life!"

**At the bar** in the Ritz, an Old Etonian is complaining to his chum, "I really don't understand, old chap. That girl from York I was dating dumped me."

"Bad luck, old man," said his chum, "But why did she dump you?"

"She said I was a posh twit," replied the Old Etonian.

"How unfair!" commiserated his chum.

"I know," said the Old Etonian, "I was so bally shocked my monocle fell out."

**Two southerners are** strolling through Workington attracting quite a bit of attention. They pass a group of jeering lads outside a chippie.

"Go home, yer posh git," shouts one of the local lads.

"I say, old chap," says one southerner to the other, "Did you hear that oik call you 'posh'?"

"I certainly did," said his chum, "But I beg to differ – just hold my top hat whilst I thrash the peasant with my shooting stick."

**It's 2008 and** a Londoner parks his car in Liverpool. He is very excited to visit as Liverpool is that year's European Capital of Culture.

"It's amazing," he remarks to his Scouser friend, "I really had no idea you people had any culture!"

The Scouser says nothing but gives him a slight smile.

The Londoner comes back two hours later to find that all the wheels have been taken off his car and it is propped up on four piles of books.

"Now you know," said the Scouser.

**Two Swindon girls,** Diane and Julie lock their keys in the Ferrari. One of the girls tries to break into the car while the other one takes pictures on her phone.

Finally Di says, "OMG! Stop taking pics, Jules, and try and help, I sooh can't get into this car!"

"Keep trying, darling," says her friend, "And jolly well hurry up – it looks like it's going to rain and the top's down."

**A man from** the fire brigade was conducting a health and safety course at an old people's home in Clacton on Sea.

He asked one old lady, "In the event of a fire, what steps would you take?"

The old lady answered, "Really big ones, me old china."

**An Essex girl** had just written off her car in a horrific accident on the M1 near Leeds. Miraculously, she managed to pry herself from the wreckage without a scratch and was applying fresh lipstick when a traffic cop arrived.

"By heck!" the officer gasped. "Your car looks like an accordion that was stomped on by an elephant. Are you OK, lass?"

"Yes, officer, I'm just fine" the Essex girl chirped.

"Well, how in the world did this happen?" the officer asked surveying the wrecked car.

"Officer, it was the strangest thing!" the Essex began. "I was driving along this road when from out of nowhere this TREE pops up in front of me. So I swerved to the right, and there was another tree! I swerved to the left and there was ANOTHER tree!

I served to the right and there was another tree! I swerved to the left and there was ...."

"Alright, lass," the officer said, cutting her off, "There's no trees on't motorway. That was your air freshener swinging back and forth."

**A taffy asks** his mate Tel from Clacton, "What's the difference between a buffalo and a bison?"

"I dunno," replied Tel, "What is the difference between a buffalo and a bison?"

"You can wash yer face in a bison, mate," replies the Welshman.

**A film crew** from Enfield were on location on in the Scottish Highlands . One day an old white-bearded Scot went up to the director and said, "Rain tomorrow."

The next day it poured.

A week later, the same old local turned up and said to director, "Storm tomorrow."

The next day there was a mighty hailstorm.

"That old bloke is absolutely incredible," said the director.

He told his secretary to hire the old man to predict the weather. However, after several successful predictions, the old fellow disappeared. The director was beside himself; the weather was changeable and he was well behind schedule. Finally the director sent a 'runner' out to search for the old man. The 'runner' returned some hours later with the venerable old man in tow. "I have to shoot a big scene tomorrow," said the director desperately, "and I'm depending on you. What will the weather be like?"

The old Scot shrugged his shoulders. "Don't know," he said. "Radio's broken."

**A man from** London and a man from Manchester are driving along the A6, one going north and one going south. It's the middle of the night and there are no other cars on the road when they hit each other head on and both cars go flying off in different directions. The Mancunian manages to climb out of his car and survey the damage. He looks at his twisted car and says, "Heck, I am really lucky to be alive!" The Londoner scrambles out of his car and looks at the wreckage. He too says to himself, "I can't believe I survived this wreck!" The man from London walks over to the man from Manchester and says, "Hey, mate, I think this is a sign that we should live as friends and harbour no hard feelings." The Mancunian thinks for a moment and says, "You know, you're absolutely right. We should be friends. Now I'm gonna see what else survived the wreck."

So he pops open his boot and finds a bottle of brandy. He says to the Londoner, "You know what, lad? I think this is another sign and we should toast to our new found understanding and friendship."

The Londoner says, "You're dead right!" and he grabs the bottle and starts swigging down the brandy. After putting away nearly half the bottle, the Londoner hands it back to the Mancunian and says, "Your turn!"

The northerner twists the cap back on the bottle and says, "Nahh, I think I'll wait for the police to show up."

**Q:** How do you make an Eton mess?

**A:** Tell him his trust fund's gone bust.

**Two businessmen were** admiring their new shop in London. It wasn't quite ready with only a few shelves set up.

One said to the other, "I bet any minute now some thick tourist is going to walk by, put his face to the window and ask what we're selling."

No sooner were the words out of his mouth when, sure enough, a curious Yorkshire man walked to the window, had a peek, and in a broad Yorkshire accent asked "What's tha sellin' ere?"

"We're selling dingbats," replied one of the Londoners sarcastically.

Without skipping a beat, the Yorkshireman said, "Tha's doing well ... Only two left!"

**A little girl** gets lost in a big shopping centre in Chelmsford. She wanders around for a while then asks one of the security guards to help her find her mummy. The security guard says to her, "What's your mum like?"

"Fags and vodka," says the little girl.

**At Catterick barracks** the Sergeant Major asks the new recruits on parade, "Does anybody here know the difference between a bread roll and a rock?"

"I do, sir!" says an eager young squaddie from Watford putting his hand up.

"Good," says the Sergeant Major, "You're cooking breakfast."

**A Chav was** given the job of painting the white lines along the M11. On his first day, he painted six miles, the next day three miles and the following day less than a mile. When the foreman asked the man why he kept painting less each day, he replied, "Ah can't do any more. Every day ah keeps getting' farther off from the jeffin' paint can."

**A Pompey walked** into a Private Investigator's Office in Glasgow holding a pencil and a piece of very thin paper.

"I want you to trace someone for me," he said to the private eye.

**A Liverpudlian walks** into a bar in London with his pit bull terrier.

"You can't bring that dog in here, mush," says the barman.

The dog seems to understand, leaps over the bar, knocks off the barman's cap and eats it.

"Get out!" the angry barman says to the scouser, "And take that dog with you. I don't like yer attitude."

"It wasn't my 'at 'e chewed," says the scouser, "it was yourn."

**A man from** Margate arrived rather late at night at a B&B in Kendal where he had made a reservation. The place was in darkness, so he knocked loudly on the door. After a long time a light appeared in an upstairs window and a woman in curlers stuck her head out, "Who are you?" she shouted bad-temperedly. "What do you want at this blooming time of night?"

"I'm staying here!" called the man.

"Stay there, then," retorted the landlady and she slammed the window shut.

**An ex-traffic warden** walks into a pizzeria in Eastbourne and orders a pizza.

The waiter asks him, "Should I cut it into six pieces or eight pieces?"

The ex-traffic warden replies, "I'm feeling right hungry, lad. You'd better cut it into eight pieces."

**A Geordie and** a Cockney are walking along the beach at Margate when the Geordie kicks a tin pot in the sand. Picking it up he starts to clean it and with a flash and a roll of thunder out pops a genie.

"Oh thank you, master. I have been trapped in that pot for ten thousand years. What is your command?"

The jealous Cockney says, "Hang on a minute, man, we're together surely we both get a wish?"

"As my Geordie master commands," says the genie.

"OK," says the Geordie, "give the bloke a wish."

"Right," says the Cockney, "I want a high wall built right around the City of London to keep all those uncouth northern so-and-sos out.

It must be twice as high as the tallest man, and strong, no weaknesses at all."

"Your wish is my command," says the genie, "now my Geordie master, what is your wish?"

"Let's get this clear, mate," says the Geordie, "a high wall, right around the city, no weaknesses, no windows, no doors, no gates, solid?"

"That's right, " says the Cockney, "Now what about your wish?"
"Easy," says the Geordie, "Fill it with water!"

**A wide boy** from Essex goes north to Kielder Forest to be a lumberjack. On his first day on the job, the boss gives him a chainsaw and says, "Listen, chum, I expect one hundred trees felled per day, if you don't make the grade you're out!"

Twelve hours later, wide boy staggers back into the camp and collapses.

"How many trees, mate?" asks the boss.

"Ninety-seven," croaks the filthy, exhausted wide boy.
The boss sees how pathetic he looks and gives him one last chance.

Next day, after thirteen hours the northerner is carried in by the other forestry workers.

"How many?" says the boss.

"Ninety-eight," says the sweaty, breathless wide boy.

Another lumberjack says, "Hey boss, that boy might be a sad specimen, but he worked non-stop for thirteen hours, no lunch, nothing!"

The boss wonders if the chainsaw might be faulty so he pulls the cord. The saw roars into life. Wide boy leaps up and shouts, "Blooming heck! What's that noise?!"

**In a fish** and chip shop restaurant in London, a Sunderland man is waiting for his meal. The woman behind the counter says, "I'm sorry for the delay with your order, love. It should be with you shortly."

The Mackem replies, "That's okay, pet, but if you don't mind me asking, what sort of bait are you using?"

**A Geordie, a** Yorkshireman, a Brummie and a man from Surrey are lost in the Sahara desert. They've been walking for days without refreshment.

"Ah'm so tired and thirsty," said the Geordie, "Ah'd kill for a pint o' broon like."

"I'm that tired and thirsty," murmured the Yorkshireman, "I could kill for a pint o' bitter."

"I'm so tired and thirsty," moaned the Brummie, "I could kill for a pint of lager."

"I'm so tired and thirsty," muttered the man from Surrey, "I really think I might be developing diabetes."

**A Mancunian walks** into a bar in Taunton and decides to wind up the barman.

"Gizza a packet of helicopter crisps, mate," he says.

"I'm sorry," the barman replies, without missing a beat, "We only have plane."

**A man in** Dagenham bought a whippet.

"What are you going to do with it, mush?" asked his friend.

"I'm going to race it," said the man.

"Oh, aye," said his friend, "By the look of it, I think you'll beat it'."

**"Son," said a** Chelsea fan to his kid as they stepped off the coach in Manchester for a big match, "Just remember, lad, it's not the winning of the game that's important…"

The boy nodded.

"… it's the drinking, fighting and setting fire to the police cars afterwards that counts."

**Q:** What do you say to a banker who has lost his hedge fund?

**A:** I'll have fries with that.

**A newspaper boy** was standing on the corner of a Edinburgh street with a stack of papers, yelling, "Read all about it. Fifty people swindled! Fifty people swindled!"

Curious, a tourist from Barnstaple walked over, bought a paper, and checked the front page. Finding nothing, the man said indignantly, "There's nothing in here about fifty people being swindled, lad."

The newspaper boy ignored him and went on, calling out, "Read all about it. Fifty-one people swindled!"

**A shy young** man from Durham visits Epsom for the weekend and goes into a smart cocktail lounge. He spots a beautiful woman sitting at the bar. After an hour of gathering up his courage, he finally goes over to her and asks tentatively, "Would you mind if I chatted to you for a while?"

The beautiful woman looks at him disdainfully and yells at the top of her voice, "NO, I WON'T GO BACK TO YOUR HOTEL WITH YOU TONIGHT!!"

Everyone in the bar is now staring at them. Naturally, the young man from Durham is hopelessly embarrassed. He slinks back to his table feeling like a real country bumpkin. After a few minutes, the beautiful woman walks over to him and smiles at him apologetically.

"I'm sorry if I embarrassed you," she says, "You see, I'm a journalist and I've got an assignment to study how people respond to embarrassing situations."

"That's OK," says the young man from Durham, then he takes a deep breath and shouts as loud as he can, "WHAT DO YOU MEAN £200?!!?"

**A Yorkshire man**, a Glaswegian and a Cornish man were sitting talking in the pub. They were comparing notes about who wore the trousers in their households.

The Yorkshire man said, "I love my wife so I let her make all the decisions."

The Glaswegian said, "Och aye, me an' me missus share everything."

"More fool you," said the Cornish man, "I tellee wat, I'm top dog at home."

"Is that right, mate?" asked the Yorkshire man.

"You control yer missus, d'ya?" asked the Glaswegian.

"I dose an' all me ansum," boasted the Cornish man, "Only t' other night me missus came to me on her hands and knees." The northerners were amazed. "What happened then?" they asked.

The Cornish man replied, "She said, 'Get out from under the bed and fight like a man'."

**At a test** match at Headingley, Yorkshire C.C. club is playing Lancaster. A cricket lover visiting from the south claps any stroke of note by either side. An elderly Yorkie turns round to him and says, "Is tha from Yorkshire?"

"No," says the cricket fan.

"Is tha from t'other side then?"

"No," says the cricket fan.

"Well," says the Yorkie crossly, "it's nowt to do with thee then."

**Q:** What do you call a cockney in a suit?

**A:** The accused.

**Q:** What's a cockney's idea of a balanced diet?

**A:** A bottle of larger in each hand.

**Overheard in a** City bar: "This credit crunch is worse than a divorce. I've lost half my net worth and I still have a wife."

**A Plymouth Argyle** fan phones up the stadium and asks, "What time is kick off?"

"Well," says the manager, "What time can you make it?"